LUCID

A POETRY COLLECTION

JYOTIRMAYA SINGH

Dedicated To My Family And Friends

Contents

Contents

Foreword

These poems originate from the twilight zone.

A space between the physical world and a higher plane.

They do not offer answers,

but echoes of a world deep inside the mind,

where human emotions blur into each other.

    If you're here, maybe you've felt that world too.

    Welcome to *Lucid*.

Preface

This book is a journey through dreams, doubts, and quiet chaos.
Some poems were written in the middle of sleepless nights,
Others during moments of silence that felt like falling.

There's no fixed theme, just fragments of scattered thoughts,
Reflections of the mind when it's most honest.

Read slowly. Feel freely.

This is **Lucid**.

Acknowledgements

To everyone who inspired me to write these poems,
And to those who are going to read them.
　　And to the version of me who kept writing when no one was reading
　　Thank you.

Prologue

This book is not meant to impress anyone.

It was written to survive a few nights, make sense of a few thoughts, and maybe leave behind something that felt real. There is no constant theme in these poems except for a journey through human emotions. These poems are meant to explore the Lucid world of human mind.

These poems came from insomnia, overthinking, quiet moments, and loud feelings. Some of them are messy. Some don't have answers. But all of them are honest.

If any of these pages feel like they were written for you.... maybe they were.

Welcome to **Lucid**.

1. Melting Walls

I fell asleep inside a question,
Woke up in a room with no wall.
The clocks were dripping from the sky,
And my name forgot how to echo.

*****

I touched the gray screams of my thoughts,
Tasted the static in mirror's gaze.
The sour light fell on my eyes,
I remained frozen and it passed days.

*****

My skin blinks with the stars,
My mind breathes with the constellations.
God whispered something to me
In the form of friendly hallucinations.

*****

I closed my eyes and fell,
Not down, but I fell inwards.
Reality caves in,
I see colors hard to put in words.

*****

Minutes bleed into colors
I can never really name.

LUCID

Gravity doesn't trust me,
The voices take the blame.

***

Time gifted me it's pocket watch,
Asked me to key it twice a day.
I met tomorrow yesterday,
Upside down sidewalks made me stray.

***

The moon poured wine in my eyes,
I see stars dancing in circles.
Reality tilted sideways,
Fog remains when the dust settles.

***

I touched the edge of sleep again,
Woke in a bed with no sky.
The poem forgot its own ending.
And so did I.

2. Mirrors Don't Lie

I stared too long again.
The mirror didn't blink.
I laughed like I was fine,
But the face inside didn't think.

***

"Back again?" it shouted.
"You always come when you're weak.
Is it guilt or shame tonight?
Or just another reason not to speak?"

***

Don't judge me like the world does,
Don't twist your lips like knives.
You know how much I've bled for silence,
You've watched all my half-lived lives.

***

"Peace?" the mirror smirked.
"You hoarded noise like gold.
Turned pain into theatre,
And called it 'just getting old.'"

***

You think I wanted this burden?
That I asked to be made hollow?

LUCID

I barely exist between deadlines
And the dread of tomorrow.

***

"You blame the world for closing in,
But you built your own cage.
You fed on poison comforts,
And now that has turned into rage."

***

I needed somewhere to run.
Even silence felt like war.
You don't know what it's like
To hear your own thoughts roar.

***

"You failed them all. You hear me?
The plans, the people, the prayers.
You chased pedestals of cloud,
Then cried when no one was there."

***

I tried, I tried. I swear I did.
Every fall I stood again.
But what do you know of courage?
You don't bleed, you just condemn.

***

"You made a god of money,
You bowed to dopamine.
Sold your soul for validation,
And bathed in gasoline."

***

I thought maybe peace lied in excess,
That pleasure might silence grief.
But the highs never embraced me,
They just offered short relief.

***

"You made art of your decay,
Wrote poems soaked in rot.
Told the world you were healing,
But healing... you were not."

***

I couldn't tell them the truth.
What if no one understood?
I lied to protect them.
That's all what I could.

***

"You call this honesty now?
Too late, too raw, too torn.
You left too many things dying,
Then wrote eulogies at dawn."

***

Maybe words are all I have left.
Maybe I deserve the ache.
But who are you to speak of truth,
When all you do is break?

***

"You always blamed the weather,
The clock, your past, your name.
But SHE left, not because of life...
She left because of your shame."

***

Don't you dare speak about her.
You don't know what we had.
You're just glass reflecting light
Do you know what it means to be sad?

***

[CRASH]

***

And I broke the mirror
To silence him, the mirror had to crack.
But shards speak louder than silence,
Now a thousand reflections stare back.

3. Finding Answers

I am hard to deal with,
I don't want to be
But that's who I am.

***

I'm an incomplete puzzle,
An unanswered riddle,
I know that I am critical.

***

People change like seasons,
They say change is the law of nature,
I believe that's an excuse.

***

I have lost the traction of time,
And the gravity of the situations.
The voices keep getting louder.

***

My existence is a lapse of reason.
I am cursed with the ability
To see behind the fake smiles.

***

Death is knocking
On the door of my house.

I've prepared a meal for it.

***

Consciousness is a curse,
A disease without cure.
The human form is limiting.

***

There is something inherently wrong
With the way we perceive ourselves.
We might be in hell but we'd never know.

***

How can optimism be real
When everything burns,
You just need enough fuel?

***

Hope is hallucination.
A figment of imagination.
Death is inevitable.

4. Paranoia

Paranoid,
So deeply paranoid,
Everything I do, anywhere I am,
Something stares from the void.

*****

Paranoid,
Walking alone at midnight.
Something's following me.
It disappears under light.

*****

Sitting in my room alone,
Not really alone, am I?
The walls are listening.
Solitude is a lie.

*****

There's someone watching
My every single movement.
I look all around, but
It hides in walls adjacent.

*****

Every time I'm in public,
I watch over my shoulder.

LUCID

My room changes when I leave,
Things feel out of order.
***

Look left, look right, then left again.
Something's hiding in the shadow.
Keeps tracking every step I take,
And fear makes time move slow.
***

I keep my eyes wide open,
Always afraid of my privacy.
The silence folds the walls in.
Someone is reading my diary.
***

The walls listen.
The doors speak at night.
The fan whispers my name.
Something moves just out of sight.
***

I notice each car in the neighborhood,
Watch every neighbor's expression.
I think someone's following me,
Their motive feels like obsession.
***

I'm so paranoid,
I check the lock three times or more.
Then I sit in silent tension,
Counting creaks upon the floor.

***

Driving.
Eyes fixed on the rearview mirror.
If one car follows too long,
The fear just keeps drawing nearer.

***

Walking.
Even shadows feel unsafe.
They trail too close behind me
As if they're waiting to replace.

***

In the mirror,
Something pretends it's me.
It knows the secrets I buried,
Knows things I swore would never be.

***

I don't trust anyone anymore.
My thoughts no longer feel my own.
Someone's read my diary,
Now I feel overthrown.

***

They stole the whole picture.
My room feels staged, not true.
Everything's out of order,
Like someone rehearsed my view.

***

LUCID

Someone read my diary,
Stole my past from me.
I am being written out
Of my own story.

5. Hey Psychiatrist

Demarcation of pale melodies
From obfuscated burning violins.
Quixotic ephemeral pleasures
Arising from pulchritudinous silence.

***

Sesquipedalian scriptures expressing
Ineffable ubiquitous glory of this realm.
Forgotten evanescent halcyon days
Filled with iridescence and petrichor.

***

Oscillating vestiges of consciousness,
Tarnished by lachrymose reverie.
Anfractuous corridors of thought
Entombed in metaphysical elegy.

***

Obsequious stars weep stardust,
A soliloquy for forgotten skies.
Mellifluous agony echoes in voids,
Clad in euphemistic disguise.

***

Funereal auroras wane and shiver
Over sepulchral vales of lore.

LUCID

Where once dwelt an effulgent heart
Now dwells an elegiac uproar.

***

Hey psychiatrist,
this is how I feel inside.
So why does no one
Understand my mind?

6. Hollow Soul

I filled a pool full of tears
Then drowned in it.
Some say my soul still haunts those waters
But people are good with rumors.
***

Carved out of stone but left hollow,
Put on a pedestal just to weather.
The nights grow darker and colder,
Humanity further strays due to its hunger.
***

The world once fit inside my fist.
Unclenched it, hoping to grow.
It slipped, like sand of hourglass,
And vanished where I couldn't go.
***

A million paintings hanging on walls,
A million songs for anyone who listens.
Why should I disappoint a world so beautiful
By my sorry existence.
***

There are more religions than I can count,
All I know is that I'm a sinner in them all.

LUCID

There's no redemption for the wicked
For he knows he shall not make it till fall.
***

Hollow souls, false prophecies and fake promises,
The trinity forging the contemporary times.
The world is already burning,
Some like to call it a morning.

7. Poet's Curse

Poet's curse,
We lose the ones we write for.
The beauty poets praise
Is the one they never got.

***

Too much trauma,
Searching answers in diaries.
Inked pages and empty pens
Just to write the perfect poem.

***

We romanticize silence,
Because no one ever stayed.
We bleed metaphors at midnight
Just to keep the ghosts obeyed.

***

The ones we loved
Live in verses they'll never read.
We inked our wounds for them.
But they were never meant to bleed.

***

I've burned my name
On every stanza I've written.

But no one's looked close enough
To see the wounds beneath the rhythm.

***

Poetry is a funeral
Where the eulogy rhymes.
We bury our feelings
But dig them up time after time.

***

I tried writing peace,
But sorrow flows easier.
The quill prefers suffering
Over happily-ever-after.

***

Poet's curse,
We lose the ones we love.
And all our poems for them
Still never feel enough.

8. What Happened

You have changed,
Your smile is now gone?
Did you leave it in a poem
You once wrote?
Did you leave it in the mirror
Then stopped looking at yourself?
Did you hide it inside a metal safe
So that nobody steals it?
Did you keep it inside a photograph
That you never look at?
You were once an amateur poet,
You used to dream of being a writer.
Life wasn't kind to you,
You had to work instead.
I can't rhyme like you do
And maybe I never should.
You used to write a diary,
Maybe you left your smile within it.
Your smile was as bright as dawn
Then you began staying up at night.
What happened? What changed?
No one broke your heart,

LUCID

You told me it was made of rock.
Why don't you rhyme anymore?
Why don't you write another poem
And post it down to the Earth?

9. Pocket Rhymes

Got nothing in my hands
But hopes and plans.
In this world of luxury sedans,
I think I'm inside minivans.

***

Been waking up tired,
Sleeping through the day.
My phone stays quiet,
But I text you anyway.

***

They ask me why I'm distant,
Why I disappear in between.
But I've seen the credits rolling
Since I turned sixteen.

***

Got nothing in return,
But lessons I didn't wanna learn.
They say everything will burn
But it's cold when the seasons turn.

***

I want it all
But I'm just mediocre.

LUCID

Posters on the wall
Still whisper 'Be better'.

***

I think I lost my mind,
Walking alone kicking rocks.
I do not like weird long talks,
I scribble thoughts on long walks.

***

Never been the loudest voice,
But I feel every word I write.
In a world chasing neon lights,
I find comfort in the night.

***

Been smuggling sunlight
Inside my old torn shoes.
Always been getting the blues
But now I got nothing to lose.

***

Not chasing love,
I believe my heart is made of stone.
Cause love, well, in the end,
I'm all alone.

***

Maybe I'm not made for gold lights,
But I still hum beneath street signs.
Got nothing in my hands, again
But I found a home in rhymes.

10. Last Night

Last night,
I lost someone
I never had.
Barely felt anything.
***

Last night,
I lost someone
I wanted so much.
I could've given everything.
***

Guess this is how
This was meant to be.
You never found out
And I never said anything.
***

I wrote some poems
Made them rhyme for you.
Forgive me or forget me,
To me, both mean nothing.
***

Last night,
A poet died quietly,

The one who wrote
Romantic verses.

***

Last night,
A poet was born again.
The one who wrote
Of horrors and miseries.

***

Last night,
A lot changed
In one life
But another never knew.

11. Monday Mournings

Man, I hate the alarm clocks,
Who wanna wake up on Mondays?
I guess I am still alive
Like smoke above old ashtrays.

***

Sent some texts to God,
He left me on read.
Sharing drinks with echoes
Inside my head.

***

Stacking apologies like bricks,
I made a house out of pain.
Yes, it hurt, I won't pretend.
But love, I'd do it all again.

***

Nightfall sonder syndrome,
Writing poems on constellations.
Wearing mismatched socks,
Stitching smiles out of hallucinations.

***

Some days I feel like TV static,
In a world stuck on rewind.

People talk but never listen,
So I just vibe with my mind.

***

I carry my past in shoeboxes,
Taped shut but never thrown.
They rattle when I walk too fast,
Like ghosts that follow me home.

***

Too many thoughts in my mind,
Some that I wanna leave behind.
You thought you could break me,
But love, I'm already hollow inside.

***

Tired of trying to be profound,
I just want to feel okay.
Put some sunlight in a jar
And save it for a rainy day.

***

I laugh like I mean it sometimes,
Even if my voice shakes.
I write about the healing
Even when everything aches.

***

Maybe peace is a secondhand coat
That don't fit but keeps me warm.
Maybe growth isn't golden light
But like a candle in a storm.

***

Feels like I only go backwards
And disappear out of sight.
But trust me when I say
That I am gonna be alright.

***

Still here, murmuring poems
On Monday mornings.

12. Euthanasia Enthusiast

They think I chase the noose,
That silence is what I choose.
But some nights, I just sit frozen,
Watching the fan spin with the blues.

***

They say I flirt with death,
Count pain like petals on the floor.
"She loves me," "She loves me not,"
Till I forget what I started for.

***

I write eulogies in rhymes,
Just to feel like I still exist.
Coffins made of quiet dreams
And feelings I used to resist.

***

Sometimes I think I wear the dark
Like those clothes I outgrew.
Inside my mind, there are places
Even sunlight won't break through.

***

Yeah, I've named the knives.
Yeah, I've weighed the fall.

But most nights, I'm just tired,
And sleep don't help at all.

***

I don't really want to vanish,
Just want the noise to slow.
Want to stop feeling like
I'm five steps behind the show.

***

Hope? That's a tricky word.
It visits like a song you skip.
But some mornings my first thought is
"Let's not lose the grip."

***

No, I ain't healed,
Just stitched in strange ways.
But I'm still here,
Still counting halfway days.

***

So if you ask what keeps me going.
It's not faith, or fate, or pride.
It's the fact that I've seen worse nights
And somehow I'm still alive.

13. Prison Inside

Go to prison,
Rediscover religion.
You never asked God for guidance,
Now your apologies await his response.

***

You justify your wreckage,
Say you have been through it all,
The lies, the knives, the losses,
Till you finally hit the wall.

***

Go to prison,
Meet your shadow at last.
It's been trailing you for years,
Dressed in the faces of your past.

***

Locked inside a cell,
Have a conversation with solitude,
She has some things to talk about,
Let the silence finally protrude.

***

Go to prison,
Let the night interrogate you.

As the moonlight splits through bars,
You will realize reality was never true.

***

You'll dream of the sins you did,
Of hands you should've held.
The guilt won't drown you.
It'll teach you how to swim in hell.

***

Go to prison,
You need some time alone.
You don't like your own company
But you still remain unknown.

***

The walls inch closer,
The cell shrinks by the day.
Regret outlive flesh, isn't it?
Apologies never find their way.

***

Go to prison.
The sentence is yours to serve.
The cell? Just your ribs.
The lock? Your own nerves.

14. Broken Gospel

Like Adam,
The first one here.
Alone but
Losing a rib is what I fear.

***

Like Eve,
Blamed for my fall.
The serpent fooled me
But sin is done by all.

***

Like Moses,
I can split open the sea
But I am afraid
Of the path to my destiny.

***

Like Abel,
Brought a gift with trembling grace.
But goodness was punished,
Left blood where none took place.

***

Like Cain,
Forced to live another day.

Death seems sweet
But it stays far away.

***

Like Judas,
My life tied in shame.
Sold my soul for rust,
Now I curse my own name.

***

Like Lazarus,
I rose when they cried.
But no one knows
How it feels to have died.

***

Like Noah
But I built my ark in vain.
The flood was inside me,
It drowned my life again.

***

Like Magdalene,
I washed the sins off Lord's feet.
But my name is stained
In every crowded street.

***

Like Peter,
Hung upside down to pray.
The guilt outweighed the cross,
Still I begged to look away.

LUCID

***

Like Bible,
I remain a mystery.
Stuck at the border
Of fiction and reality.

15. A Letter To Aphrodite

Aphrodite, queen of love,
The sky and the oceans call out your name.
The poets write of you in gold,
But love still fades, it dies the same.
***

They say your beauty shapes the world,
That hearts will fall at your command.
But tell me, Aphrodite, if that's true,
Why does love slip right through my hand?
***

You bring desire, joy, and light,
But love has been such a cruel disguise.
Even though you shine in endless grace,
I only see her when I close my eyes.
***

She studies with me, she knows my name,
Yet doesn't know the way I feel.
She isn't you, she has no throne,
But still, her presence feels unreal.
***

Her hair is dark, her smile is soft,
Her voice is quiet, but it stays.
She doesn't have a halo like you,
But I am lost within her gaze.

***

No doves take flight when she walks by,
No myths were written in her name.
But when she laughs, the world feels right,
And nothing else will feel the same.

***

Aphrodite, hear my words,
If love is truly yours to guide,
Then whisper softly in her ear,
And let her heart stay by my side.

***

Let autumn leaves spell out my words,
Let winter winds repeat my name.
Let her remember who I am,
Let her feel my love the same.

***

But if she stays beyond my reach,
If fate decides this love should die,
Then tell me, goddess, what is love,
If it is meant to end with a goodbye?

***

You are the one they pray to most,
The goddess lovers believe to be true.

You might be the symbol of love,
Alas! I love her, not you.

16. An Apology To Aphrodite

I carved altars for a ghost,
Offered prayers to an empty throne.
Built pedestals of unwritten psalms
For a muse who left me alone.

***

Hey Aphrodite, it's me again,
Barefoot at your ancient shrine.
The boy who begged for her heart,
Now begs to reclaim what was mine.

***

I mistook her silence for softness,
Mistook her smile for a vow.
I praised her like a goddess,
But she was never you. I see that now.

***

You warned me in quiet omens,
In sunsets that died too fast.
But I was lost in illusion,
Writing futures from a shattered past.

***

I once asked the autumn to spell my name,
Now those leaves decay in my heart.
Even my verses have turned against me,
They ask if I was meant to be hurt.

***

She was no divine reflection.
Only a shadow dressed in light.
But I called her sacred scripture,
And embraced the lie each night.

***

I mocked your golden throne for her,
Called her grace the almighty of mine.
But your silence was not cruelty.
It was mercy, misread as decline.

***

Now every metaphor feels bitter,
Each stanza crawls beneath my skin.
My ink once bloomed with yearning,
Now it scars and recounts my sin.

***

I offer no roses this time,
No hymns, no sacred rhyme.
Only the truth. I chose the wrong star,
And crashed long before my climb.

***

Forgive me, Aphrodite,
For confusing beauty with devotion.

LUCID

For chasing a ripple
And mistaking it for an ocean.

***

Forgive me, Aphrodite,
I sought in fragile flesh
What only gods define
When the stars align.

***

Forgive me, Aphrodite,
I wrote, "I loved her, not you."
But in the ruins of that line,
It's your silence that saw me through.

17. Elegy Of Love

I'd send you flowers
But they wilt.
***

Never knew I had a heart,
Still, you took it away.
The city called me heartless,
But who cares what they say.
***

I'd write you a symphony
But the music fades.
***

I had a heart of rock,
You broke it anyway.
I always knew your game
But I'd let you play.
***

I'd build you a castle
But they fall.
***

You etched your name
Inside my mind's wall.
I lit the match for warmth,

LUCID

You watched the flames enthrall.

***

I'd kill for you,
But you hate murders.

***

I liked silence,
You wanted fun.
You just witnessed my war,
And said that you were done.

***

I'd give you truth
But you'd call it hate.

***

You asked for poetry
But never read a page.
You smiled like a sunrise
That held me like a cage.

***

I'd hold your hands
But your hands held the world.

***

You loved like lightning,
Brief, and never dull.
Now I'm just static,
Fading after the trouble.

***

JYOTIRMAYA SINGH

I'd give you silence
But you'd scream instead.
***

I buried my voice
Where your name once bled.
Our story's grave is shallow,
But the words stay dead.
***

I'd send you forgiveness
But I'm out of grace.
***

I gave you a mirror
You shattered my face.
I followed you everywhere,
You led me to this hellish place.
***

I'd give you my end
But you'd write a start.
***

So take this poem,
And leave with my heart.
Nomad soul.
I'm too far gone to be hurt.

18. Heart Shaped Coffin

I watched you fall for people
who never saw your light.
And I kept building stories
just to kill them overnight.

***

You stayed silent but I kept
Every word you never said.
I stitched together conversations
from the echoes inside my head.

***

I wrote you into poems
you'll never read or hear.
You lived inside my verses
but were you ever near?

***

I lost someone I never had,
Mistakes were made from my end
For thinking of you
As something more than a friend.

***

I keep your ghost in my poems,
Hoping one day I'd get over you.

It's my fate to leave in the end,
You are just someone I once knew.

***

So I'll dig a grave in silence,
beneath the poems I wrote in sin.
And bury all my love for you
in a heart-shaped coffin.

19. Dream Resident

In the nights, when I fall too deep,
I stumble into a place beyond sleep.
A realm sewn from forgotten skies,
Where stars flicker like blinking eyes.

***

There, she waits.... soft, serene,
A girl I know, yet have never seen.
Her face, a blur of gentle flame,
But every time I ask, she hides her name.

***

They say dreams are feeble, fleeting,
But she's constant. She always meets me
Where the moon hums backwards
And oceans bloom from broken jars.

***

Her voice? A melody I can never hum.
A lullaby brewed from opium.
Her touch? Like candlelight underwater.
Familiar. Fragile. Straying further.

***

I've loved her for a thousand nights,
Yet never once caught her in daylight.

She laughs like clockwork breaking apart,
Leaves footprints like question marks.

***

Her dress flows like spilled ink,
Feet never touch the ground.
Her shadow walks a second late,
And fades when I get around.

***

I ask her, "Why don't I know your face?"
She smiles... like mirrors bending space.
"Your waking mind was never built
To carry something born of silk."

***

She holds my hand like a promise torn,
Whispers secrets the stars have sworn.
Her eyes... two moons spinning slow,
Contain every answer I'll never know.

***

The sky behind her flickers red,
Planets bloom, then play dead.
In dream realm, time's rules bend
Still, I know this world will end.

***

Right before I wake, she turns,
As if she knows it's my time to return.
She steps back with a heavy hush.
My heartbeat builds, reality rush.

***

She never fights the ending,
Just vanishes in cyan steam.
My room returns. I blink. I stare.
Alone again, with midnight air.

***

The day resumes in colorless hues,
But her voice lingers like residue.
Not her face, not her name.
Just her rhythm inside my brain.

***

She is the love I'll never remember,
A song I hum but can't deliver.
And every time I wake, I ache
For the one my memory can't remake.

***

You ask why I return each night?
Because in her world, wrong feels right.
She forgets the rules. I forget the pain.
And there, I'm whole... I'm sane.

***

Reality clings to faces and frames,
But dreams... they only remember names.
And hers, if I ever knew it
Is the only thing I'd never forget.

20. Dinner With Timekeeper

The table was longer than the sky,
Yet somehow folded like paper.
Salt and pepper floated midair,
Spinning slowly, straying further.

***

The ceiling was a melting mirror,
Reflecting dreams I hadn't caught.
The clouds danced in Van Gogh strokes,
Each one spelling things I forgot.

***

The sun and moon were lovers,
Getting closer with each breath.
The tablecloth pulsed like a heart,
Its patterns shifting. Birth, then death.

***

The soup smelled like forgotten lullabies,
Swirled in colors I couldn't name.
The spoon bent at uncanny angles,
Still, it never stirred the same.

***

The bread was hollow,
But hummed when I broke it.
A cheap mimic of a meal,
Like comfort dreamt by a poet.

***

The dish in front looked... almost right.
Chicken, perhaps, with a porcelain glaze.
But the shadows it cast were moving,
And it moved once through the haze.

***

The wine was ink and blood mixed,
The napkins folded like white moths.
The chairs creaked in fluent Morse code,
Reciting verses of ancient thoughts.

***

And across from me sat a man.
No, a shape, something near.
Slender frame in a three piece suit,
His presence fed every fear.

***

His skin was pale, his fingers grey,
Wearing time like jewelry.
A pocket watch clung to his throat,
Ticking in every century.

***

His face was blank,no eyes, no lips,
Just a whitewashed canvas.

But his voice cracked through the silence
Like thunder stitched into abyss.
***

He raised a hand and offered food,
Motioned gently toward my plate.
I looked down at the uncanny soup.
And something behind it whispered, "Wait."
***

"Who... are you?" I finally spoke.
"And what is this you're offering me?"
My voice felt distant, like borrowed static,
My hands twitching nervously.
***

"I am the Timekeeper," he replied.
His voice echoed, but face stood still.
"I've come to collect your dues.
What you owe me, you owe by will."
***

"Dues?" I asked, afraid of my life.
"What do you mean? What debt?"
My heartbeat echoed his ticking watch,
My palms poured unseen sweat.
***

"Calm yourself," he said quite softly.
"Eat first. It helps it all feel right.
You owe me your wasted days,
The ones you fed to sleepless nights."

***

I stared in fear. "But how... how much?
And how do I pay for such a thing?"
My chair felt bolted to the stars,
The wine slowly began to sing.

***

He chuckled.... or the room did.
"Thirty years, give or take," he said.
"You'll pay by living through them.
No shortcuts. No dying instead."

***

I couldn't breathe. The world warped.
The sky outside began to bend.
The walls closed in with whispering clocks.
Would this madness never end?

***

I woke up in my trembling bed,
The knife still resting on my hand.
The clock read 4:03 AM.
I didn't move, but I could stand.

***

Maybe... I won't end it yet,
Not tonight, not this time.
I've got thirty years to wander through
Might as well make that debt mine.

21. Hidden In Plain Sight

How do I survive the silence inside?
Every thought is a scream I hide.
Lost in smoke and shattered mirrors,
Past is consumed by phantom terrors.

***

How do you ignore the loud silence?
Every night becomes a cage of knives.
Lost between dead hopes and dreams,
Past is where my darkness thrives.

***

Hope is just a cruel disguise,
Eyes dry, but the soul still cries.
Lurking under the skin so pale,
Promises rot as they fail.

***

High on the pain,
End of life seems near.
Lying to myself now and then,
Paper cuts make vision clear.

***

Howling winds echo inside my head,
Even my shadow refuse to die.

LUCID

Let my blood become the ink,
Pages shiver, they scream, they sink.
***

Holding on to the frail will to live,
Even silence screams spells.
Leave me alone to suffer,
Poisoned thoughts, I feel better.

22. A Nomad In The Night

The undressed moonlight
Reveals another face of the night.
Whispers to the men on chessboard
About the marbled world's Lord.

***

Midnight wears silence as perfume
While faded stars flicker in gloom.
The moon weeps in silver,
The dark nights, it won't remember.

***

Clouds stitched to blind the stars,
But the night still weeps.
The fog speaks forgotten tongues
While the streetlamp sleeps.

***

The owls chant riddles
Only the dead can solve.
When the night lowers its veil
It only asks mortals to evolve.

***

LUCID

Darkness is not a void
Just full of what we can't remember.
The rains continue the prayer
Left unfinished by clergy member.

***

The earth keeps the dead closer,
It lets the mortals stray.
Light and dark made a pact,
They let Nomad souls play.

***

My footsteps won't disturb
The old secrets in the soil.
I am a mere poet. An observer.
In this world filled by turmoil.

23. Quo Vadis?

Vita Asphyxiat

***

Living beneath a borrowed sky,
Every day living the same lie.
Same steps, same faces, same noise
This world offers but illusion of choice.

***

Old goals vanish as they arrive,
New ones echo the same old lie.
The clock restarts under our skin
Through repetition, rust, and sin.

***

We are cattle of slaughter,
Meant to die sooner or later.
Existence is a mirror that never breaks,
Filling daily with the same mistakes.

***

Fugit Tempus

***

Everyday passes exactly the same,
Days give perpetual struggle a name.
The calendar changes but we remain,

A cycle of joyless, ghosted pain.

***

Memories blur into forgotten dates,
Milestones crumble beneath our weight.
Tomorrow is yesterday in disguise,
Wearing the same tired, borrowed eyes.

***

A perpetual cycle of misery
Repeating itself since history.
Everything remains the same,
Time just burns under the flame.

***

Ad Nihilum

***

Where do we go when dreams collapse?
Each step retraces past gaps.
A finish line that folds in layers of dust,
A future built on figments of fragile trust.

***

We strive for what we can't define,
While marching on a downward line.
We all walk the same way
That leads to death and decay.

***

We chase, we fall, we rise, we flee,
A vicious cycle dressed as destiny.
The world will end in silent stone,

And no one will make it out alone.

***

Veritas Abscondita

***

The truth is quiet, yet it screams,
A voice that hijacks all our dreams.
My body, a prison; my mind, a war;
My shadow whispers more and more.

***

Mirrors lie with practiced grace,
Even God feels out of place.
What do you do when prayers return
Like knives disguised in incense burn?

***

The world is suffocating,
It has no space for living.
A pulse can mimic the will to strive,
But silence knows who's not alive

***

Via Solitaria

***

So I abandoned what I knew,
The loops, the gods, the world askew.
Walked away from names and codes,
From shallow graves that corrode.

***

I took the road where silence grows,
Where no destiny seems close.
Where the rules of existence bend,
Towards an end I cannot comprehend.

***

Yes, I walk alone, but free,
Outside the chains of history.
If there's no map, I won't be found,
But in this path, my peace is crowned.

***

Quo Vadis?

***

I remember I was conflicted
When materialism slowly faded.
I chose the road no footprints fell,
It might go to heaven or to hell.

***

I walked away from my destiny
To break the cycle of misery.
The cycle is broken but at what cost,
Everything I stood for is now lost.

***

I will keep walking till I end,
A soul unclaimed by foe or friend.
Two roads diverged, the poets lied
There's only one: the one you bide.

***

At the price of name and face,
I broke the cycle, left no trace.

24. Lost In Translation

There's a story lost in translation,
She sold happiness in glass jars.
I counted days like loose change,
The space between us got strange.

***

Carrying her memory in a paper bag
Marked 'Fragile'.
My mistake was the hope I misplaced,
Eventually got replaced.

***

The curse of a poet,
I lose the people I write for.
Sunlight can't enlighten my soul,
Everything lost, I lost control.

***

Even silence gets loud
When you've got no one to listen.
I try to make them understand
But they say 'Be a man'.

***

Not everyone leaves with goodbye,
Some just stop looking at you the same.

You took the road, I took the echo,
Now I'm hitchhiking in your shadow.

***

Anyways, it all ended
Before it even began.
You won't remember me
And I won't forget the pain.

***

I'm used to people changing
And changing people.
I'm hitchhiking through your shadow,
I'm still walking... just not toward you.

25. Metronome Home

Haven't seen dawn in ages
But I heard sky's still blue.
I captured sunlight in a jar,
Insured against the winter.

***

TV static ticks like metronome,
I hum in major keys all along.
My dreams don't fit in a suitcase,
I'd rather brew them into a song.

***

Slow summer,
Nothing changes but the calendar,
Healing feels like a song
Whose melody I barely remember.

***

Making paper boats out of receipts,
Then I sail them in the sink-sea.
I don't chase my dreams, I just
walk beside 'em, hope they notice me.

***

I've been talking to silence
And it's finally talking back.

Wearing mismatched socks
Cause life's not just white and black.

***

I found peace in coffee and books,
Blessed to be unstressed.
Writing my name on constellations
Before I finally go to bed.

***

The moonlight smokes with me,
I like the stars for company.
Healed.
Love, you never broke me,
I ain't careless just carefree.

26. Have Beens And Could Have Beens

Let's have a toast
To those who have been.
Once the shine of Venus,
Now rusted is their skin.

***

To the ones who knew
Every freckle, every scar,
Now scroll past their name
Like strangers from afar.

***

To the ones who laughed
With eyes too soft to lie,
Now drink alone at midnight
Never said goodbye.

***

To the ones who stayed
Through struggles of nether,
Now lie in separate worlds,
Still dreaming they're together.

***

To the ones who write
The love they never spoke,
Who kiss memories in their poems
And breathe in hearts they broke.

***

Let's have a toast,
For they still bleed unseen.
Once the shine of Venus,
Now lost where love has been.

***

Let's have a toast
To those who could've been.
They try to hide
But still love burns within.

***

To the ones who stayed up
Counting miles, not stars,
Whose dreams met halfway
But lived behind bars.

***

To the ones who hugged
Like goodbyes were a crime,
Whose calendars mocked them
With the passage of time.

***

To the ones who stare
At old chats, unsent,

LUCID

Each word a prayer
That never went.

***

To the ones whose names
Still tremble on lips,
But life placed oceans
Between their fingertips.

***

Let's have a toast
To those who could've been.
They carry a love
This world won't let in.

27. Broken Messiah

Took too long to understand
Real eyes realise real lies.
Real life hitchhikes too well
On this highway to hell.

***

I run as fast as I can
But karma keeps catching up.
Running from my past, I always fail.
How can I rest when the ship has set sail?

***

It is too late for apologies
When you've been living in fantasies.
Living life on borrowed time,
The clocks tick faster. No one believes.

***

Masochist melancholy maruads morale,
Misery maximises, men mask morals.
Mayhem maculates Magnificent marvel.
My most macabre malice remains immortal.

***

Eclipse on the horizon of optimism,
Graphic reality unveils horrors unseen.

LUCID

The blood signed pact still testifies
What the deal at crossroads implies.

***

When damnation was clearly visible,
I was already going insane.
Once you dance with Lucy,
You don't dance again....

28. Fade Again

Still floating in the sky,
Falling through the universe
While trying to rhyme
One stanza at a time.

***

Lucid dreaming,
Life's easier when nothing's at stake.
Such a sacrificial life,
Let the fabric of reality break.

***

End of a journey,
The darkness is familiar now,
The void knows our name,
The silence is still left to claim.

***

The backward talking fog
And owls speaking in riddles.
Aphrodite's abandoned throne
And the paranoia finally settles.

***

The final nail on the coffin
Of the rigid rules of reality.

We broke through consciousness
Into the realm of lucidity.

***

Quo vadis?
This part of our journey ends.
I hope to see you again.
The lucid poetries still remain.

***

So, this is where the sky collapses,
And ink outlives the hand.
Fade again, dear reader .
In dreams, we'll understand.

www.ingramcontent.com/pod-product-compliance
Lightning Source LLC
Chambersburg PA
CBHW020642160726
47991CB00003B/983